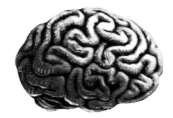

EmotionalIntelligence Appraisal™

THERE IS MORE THAN IQ

Me Edition™

My evaluation.

Name: _____

Date: _____

Published by:

DEVELOP TALENT · PROFIT SMART

www.TalentSmart.com

About the authors:

Drs. Bradberry and Greaves are authors of best selling assessments and books that bring important concepts to life quickly and easily. They wrote the Emotional Intelligence Quickbook and coauthored the Foundations of Leadership Assessment™ with Ken Blanchard—the best selling business author of all time. The Emotional Intelligence Appraisal™ has been featured in T+D Magazine, Sales and Marketing Management, Business Outlook, and Learning and Training Innovations, among others.

Travis Bradberry, Ph.D., is a leading expert on emotional intelligence and leadership who speaks on these topics internationally. Dr. Bradberry is the president and cofounder of TalentSmart who oversees new product development and the formation of alliances with strategic business partners.

Jean Greaves, Ph.D., is the CEO and cofounder of TalentSmart and an expert in emotional intelligence and strategic organizational change. Since 1989 she has helped public and private organizations with large-scale strategic change, and is responsible for the vision, values and strategic direction of TalentSmart.

At TalentSmart we strive to use the most environmentally friendly paper stocks available. Our publications are printed on acid-free recycled stock paper. Our paper always meets or exceeds the minimum GPO and EPA requirements.

Contact TalentSmart directly for discounts on bulk quantities and inquiries about training and eLearning in emotional intelligence at (888) 818-SMART.

CONTENTS

INTRODUCTION

The Emotional Intelligence Appraisal™ provides you with a complete picture of your emotional intelligence. This includes an understanding of:

- what emotional intelligence is.
- your overall emotional intelligence score.
- your current skill levels in the four areas that make up emotional intelligence.
- specific recommendations for action you can take to improve your emotional intelligence.

Before You Begin

This appraisal will ask you specific questions about your behavior. Your responses to these questions will be for your eyes only. A true reflection of your emotional intelligence skills depends on your willingness to accurately rate yourself. This requires a lot of thought into how you behave in many situations, not just the ones you handle well.

When you read each question, follow these instructions to get the most from the Emotional Intelligence Appraisal™.

1. Create a clear picture in your mind of how you think and behave in different situations.
2. Then answer honestly how often you demonstrate the behavior in question.
3. Ignore the shaded areas. You will use those later for scoring.
4. Have fun!

EMOTIONAL INTELLIGENCE APPRAISAL QUESTIONS: PART ONE

For each question, check one box according to how often you...

	Never	Rarely	Sometimes	Usually	Almost Always	Always
(1) are confident in your abilities.						
(2) admit your shortcomings.						
(3) understand your emotions as they happen.						
(4) recognize the impact your behavior has upon others.						
(5) realize when others influence your emotional state.						
Scoring area for questions 1 through 5 only						
(6) play a part in creating the difficult circumstances you encounter.						

	Never	Rarely	Sometimes	Usually	Almost Always	Always
(7) can be counted on.						
(8) handle stress well.						
(9) embrace change early on.						
(10) tolerate frustration without getting upset.						
(11) consider many options before making a decision.						
(12) strive to make the most out of situations, whether good or bad.						
(13) resist the desire to act or speak when it will not help the situation.						
Scoring area for questions 7 through 13 only						
(14) do things you regret when upset.						
(15) brush people off when something is bothering you.						
Scoring area for questions 14 through 15 only						

EMOTIONAL INTELLIGENCE APPRAISAL QUESTIONS: PART TWO

For each question, check one box according to how often you...

	Never	Rarely	Sometimes	Usually	Almost Always	Always
(16) are open to feedback.						
(17) recognize other people's feelings.						
(18) accurately pick up on the mood in the room.						
(19) hear what the other person is "really" saying.						
Scoring area for questions 16 through 19 only						
(20) are withdrawn in social situations.						

	Never	Rarely	Sometimes	Usually	Almost Always	Always
(21) directly address people in difficult situations.						
(22) get along well with others.						
(23) communicate clearly and effectively.						
(24) show others you care what they are going through.						
(25) handle conflict effectively.						
(26) use sensitivity to another person's feelings to manage interactions effectively.						
(27) learn about others in order to get along better with them.						
Scoring area for questions 21 through 27 only						
(28) explain yourself to others.						

SCORING YOUR RESULTS: SELF-AWARENESS SCORE

Congratulations, your survey is complete. You will now score your results in four small parts. Begin here with the first part, which consists of questions 1-6 on page five.

Step One: For questions 1-5 only, add up the number of checks in each column and write the totals in the shaded area directly below question #5 on page five. Transfer this directly to the shaded area of Column A on this page.

Step Two: In the non-shaded area of Column A on this page, enter a 1 next to the response you chose for question #6 on page five.

Step Three: Multiply *each row* of Column A by the number directly next to it in Column B. Write the answer for each row in Column C.

Step Four: Add up all the numbers in Column C and write the answer on the line next to the phrase "Total Column C."

		COLUMN A	COLUMN B	COLUMN C
QUESTIONS 1-5	Never		X 1	
	Rarely		X 2	
	Sometimes		X 3	
	Usually		X 4	
	Almost Always		X 5	
	Always		X 6	
QUESTION 6	Never		X 1	
	Rarely		X 2	
	Sometimes		X 3	
	Usually		X 5	
	Almost Always		X 6	
	Always		X 4	

Total Column C = _____

Step Five: Find your total from Column C in the left-hand column of one of the tables to the right. Circle the number directly to the right of it. The number you circle is your Self-Awareness score. Self-Awareness is one of the four skills that make up emotional intelligence.

Step Six: Write your Self-Awareness score in the table on page 11.

Column C	Self-Awareness	Column C	Self-Awareness
6-7	10	22	74
8	14	23	76
9	21	24	77
10	26	25	79
11	33	26	82
12	39	27	83
13	46	28	85
14	52	29	86
15	58	30	89
16	61	31	90
17	64	32	92
18	67	33	94
19	70	34	96
20	72	35	98
21	73	36	100

SCORING YOUR RESULTS: SELF-MANAGEMENT SCORE

Now it's time to score the next part of your results. This section covers questions 7-15 on page five.

Step One: For questions 7-13 only, add up the number of checks in each column and write the totals in the shaded area directly below question #13 on page five. Transfer this directly to the shaded area of Column D on this page.

Step Two: For questions 14-15 only, add up the number of checks in each column and write the totals in the shaded area directly below question #15. Transfer this directly to the non-shaded area of Column D on this page.

Step Three: Multiply *each row* of Column D by the number directly next to it in Column E. Write the answer for each row in Column F.

Step Four: Add up all the numbers in Column F and write the answer on the line next to the phrase "Total Column F."

Step Five: Find your total from Column F in the left-hand column of one of the tables to the right. Circle the number directly to the right of it. The number you circle is your Self-Management score. Self-Management is one of the four skills that make up emotional intelligence.

Step Six: Write your Self-Management score in the table on page 11.

		COLUMN D	COLUMN E	COLUMN F
QUESTIONS 7-13	Never		X 1	
	Rarely		X 2	
	Sometimes		X 3	
	Usually		X 4	
	Almost Always		X 5	
	Always		X 6	
QUESTIONS 14-15	Never		X 6	
	Rarely		X 5	
	Sometimes		X 4	
	Usually		X 3	
	Almost Always		X 2	
	Always		X 1	

Total Column F = _____

Column F	Self-Management	Column F	Self-Management	Column F	Self-Management
9-10	10	25	39	40	78
11	13	26	40	41	80
12	15	27	45	42	82
13	16	28	49	43	85
14	18	29	52	44	87
15	20	30	55	45	91
16	21	31	58	46	92
17	23	32	62	47	93
18	26	33	65	48	94
19	28	34	68	49	95
20	31	35	71	50	96
21	33	36	73	51	97
22	34	37	74	52	98
23	36	38	75	53	99
24	37	39	76	54	100

SCORING YOUR RESULTS: SOCIAL AWARENESS SCORE

Now score the third part of your results, questions 16-20 on page six.

Step One: For questions 16-19 only, add up the number of checks in each column and write the totals in the shaded area directly below question #19 on page six. Transfer this directly to the shaded area of Column G on this page.

Step Two: In the non-shaded portion of Column G, enter a 1 next to the response you chose for question #20.

Step Three: Multiply *each row* of Column G by the number directly next to it in Column H. Write the answer for each row in Column I.

Step Four: Add up all the numbers in Column I and write the answer on the line next to the phrase "Total Column I."

		COLUMN G	COLUMN H	COLUMN I
QUESTIONS 16-19	Never		X 1	
	Rarely		X 2	
	Sometimes		X 3	
	Usually		X 4	
	Almost Always		X 5	
	Always		X 6	
QUESTION 20	Never		X 5	
	Rarely		X 6	
	Sometimes		X 4	
	Usually		X 3	
	Almost Always		X 2	
	Always		X 1	

Total Column I = _____

Step Five: Find your total from Column I in the left-hand column of one of the tables to the right. Circle the number directly to the right of it. The number you circle is your Social Awareness score. Social Awareness is one of the four skills that make up emotional intelligence.

Step Six: Write your Social Awareness score in the table on page 11.

Column I	Social Awareness	Column I	Social Awareness
5	10	18	70
6	15	19	72
7	20	20	74
8	25	21	76
9	32	22	77
10	40	23	79
11	47	24	81
12	54	25	88
13	58	26	90
14	62	27	92
15	64	28	93
16	65	29	96
17	68	30	100

SCORING YOUR RESULTS: RELATIONSHIP MANAGEMENT SCORE

Now it's time to score the last part of your results. This covers questions 21-28 on page six.

Step One: For questions 21-27 only, add up the number of checks in each column and place the totals in the shaded area directly below question #27 on page six. Transfer this directly to the shaded area of Column J on this page.

Step Two: In the non-shaded portion of Column J, enter a 1 next to the response you chose for question #28.

Step Three: Multiply *each row* of Column J by the number directly next to it in Column K. Write the answer for each row in Column L.

Step Four: Add up all the numbers in Column L and write the answer on the line next to the phrase "Total Column L."

		COLUMN J	COLUMN K	COLUMN L
QUESTIONS 21-27	Never		X 1	
	Rarely		X 2	
	Sometimes		X 3	
	Usually		X 4	
	Almost Always		X 5	
	Always		X 6	
QUESTION 28	Never		X 1	
	Rarely		X 2	
	Sometimes		X 3	
	Usually		X 4	
	Almost Always		X 6	
	Always		X 5	

Total Column L = _____

Step Five: Find your total from Column L in the left-hand column of one of the tables to the right. Circle the number directly to the right of it. The number you circle is your Relationship Management score. Relationship Management is one of the four skills that make up emotional intelligence.

Step Six: Write your Relationship Management score in the table on page 11.

Column L	Relationship Management
8	10
9	13
10	17
11	19
12	21
13	22
14	25
15	27
16	29
17	30
18	32
19	36
20	39
21	43

Column L	Relationship Management
22	45
23	48
24	50
25	53
26	56
27	57
28	59
29	61
30	65
31	67
32	70
33	71
34	73
35	75

Column L	Relationship Management
36	77
37	78
38	80
39	83
40	84
41	86
42	87
43	89
44	91
45	93
46	95
47	96
48	100

MY EMOTIONAL INTELLIGENCE SCORES
Emotional intelligence is made up of four skills.

- Write each of your skill scores in the following table. They are the numbers you **circled** at the bottom of pages 7-10.
- Add the four skill scores and place the value next to where it says, *"Total of Skill Scores."*
- Find your total in the left-hand column of one of the tables below. The number directly next to it, in the right-hand column, is your overall emotional intelligence (EQ) score. Be sure to circle your score and write it in the Overall EQ Score box.

Skill Score

SELF-AWARENESS	
SELF-MANAGEMENT	
SOCIAL AWARENESS	
RELATIONSHIP MANAGEMENT	

Total of Skill Scores = _____

OVERALL EQ SCORE

Sum of Skill Scores	Overall EQ Score	Sum of Skill Scores	Overall EQ Score	Sum of Skill Scores	Overall EQ Score
40-48	10	259-262	65	331-334	83
49-68	15	263-266	66	335-337	84
69-88	20	267-270	67	338-341	85
89-108	25	271-273	68	342-344	86
109-128	30	274-277	69	345-348	87
129-148	35	278-281	70	349-352	88
149-167	40	282-285	71	353-356	89
168-187	45	286-289	72	357-360	90
188-203	50	290-293	73	361-364	91
204-211	52	294-297	74	365-368	92
212-219	54	298-301	75	369-372	93
220-227	56	302-305	76	373-376	94
228-238	58	306-309	77	377-380	95
239-242	60	310-313	78	381-385	96
243-246	61	314-318	79	386-389	97
247-250	62	319-323	80	390-393	98
251-254	63	324-326	81	394-396	99
255-258	64	327-330	82	397-400	100

EMOTIONAL INTELLIGENCE APPRAISAL™

WHAT THE SCORES MEAN

Scores on the Emotional Intelligence Appraisal™ come from a "normed sample." That means your scores are based on a comparison to tens of thousands of responses to discover where you fall relative to the general population. Read the following descriptions to better understand what your scores mean about your current skill level.

SCORE	MEANING
90-100	**A STRENGTH TO CAPITALIZE ON** These scores are much higher than average and indicate a noteworthy strength. These strengths probably come naturally to you, or exist because you have worked hard to develop them. Seize every opportunity to use these emotionally intelligent behaviors to maximize your success. You are highly competent in this skill, so work to capitalize on it and achieve your potential.
80-89	**A STRENGTH TO BUILD ON** This score is above average. However, there are a few situations where you don't demonstrate emotionally intelligent behavior. There are many things you are doing well to have received this score and a few that could be better with some practice. Study the behaviors for which you received this score and consider how you can polish your skills.
70-79	**WITH A LITTLE IMPROVEMENT, THIS COULD BE A STRENGTH** You are aware of some of the behaviors for which you received this score and you are doing well. Other emotionally intelligent behaviors in this group are holding you back. Lots of people start here and see big improvement in their emotional intelligence once it's brought to their attention. Use this opportunity to discover your potential and improve in the areas where you don't do as well.
60-69	**SOMETHING YOU SHOULD WORK ON** This is an area where you sometimes demonstrate emotionally intelligent behavior but not usually. You may be starting to let people down. Perhaps this is a skill that doesn't always come naturally for you or that you don't use. With a little improvement in this skill, your credibility will go way up.
59 or below	**A CONCERN YOU MUST ADDRESS** This skill area is either a problem for you, you don't value it or you didn't know it was important. The bad news is your skills in this area are limiting your effectiveness. The good news about this discovery and choosing to do something about it is it will go a long way toward improving your emotionally intelligent behavior.

"Emotions have taught mankind to reason."
- Vauvenargues

WHAT IS EMOTIONAL INTELLIGENCE?

Learning about emotional intelligence (EQ) will help you to make use of your scores and discover how you can improve your EQ. Emotional intelligence comes down to four key skills.

The first two skills focus on you.

(1) **Self-Awareness:** Your ability to accurately perceive your own emotions and stay aware of them as they happen. This includes keeping on top of how you tend to respond to specific situations and people.

(2) **Self-Management:** Your ability to use awareness of your emotions to stay flexible and positively direct your behavior. This means managing your emotional reactions to all situations and people.

The last two skills focus more on your contact with other people.

(3) **Social Awareness:** Your ability to accurately pick up on emotions in other people and get what is really going on. This often means understanding what other people are thinking and feeling even if you don't feel the same way.

(4) **Relationship Management:** Your ability to use your awareness of your emotions and the emotions of others to manage interactions successfully. This includes clear communication and effectively handling conflict.

What Does Emotional Intelligence Look Like?

The four skills of emotional intelligence are based on a connection between what you see and what you do with yourself and others.

	WHAT I SEE	WHAT I DO
WITH ME	Self-Awareness	Self-Management
WITH OTHERS	Social Awareness	Relationship Management

UNDERSTANDING YOUR EMOTIONAL INTELLIGENCE

Use this graph to map a picture of your EQ. Enter your skill scores from page 11 on the line under their names. Do the same for your overall EQ score. Plot a point on the graph for each of your emotional intelligence skills and your overall EQ score. Connect these points with a line to visualize your current level of emotional intelligence.

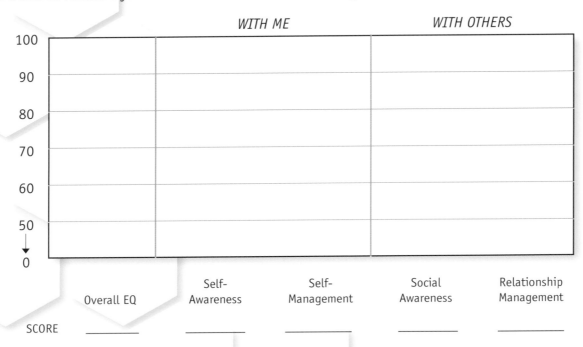

What trends do you see in your graph? Look for the following...

1. **Your Tendency:** Is your EQ higher *WITH ME* or *WITH OTHERS*?   (circle one)   WITH ME   WITH OTHERS

2. **Your Strength:** Which skill score is your highest?   _____

3. **Your Weakness:** Which skill score is your lowest?   _____

Looking Forward

Use these trends to help you set goals on the following page. You may choose to build a strength, develop a weakness or both.

SETTING MY EQ DEVELOPMENT GOALS

Fill in this page to help define what you want to work on to develop your emotional intelligence skills.

When it comes to EQ, I'm already good at...

_____

_____

_____

_____

I could improve...

_____

_____

_____

_____

My EQ development goals...

_____

_____

_____

"What lies behind us and what lies before us are
tiny matters compared to what lies within us."
— Oliver Wendell Holmes

IMPROVING EMOTIONAL INTELLIGENCE

Emotional intelligence is very different from regular intelligence.

- With regular intelligence, it is understood that you are generally as "smart" now as you are ever going to be. People learn new facts but their intelligence, or their ability to learn, remains largely the same.

Emotional intelligence is a flexible skill that can be readily learned.

- People actually increase their emotional intelligence by working on the skills outlined in this feedback report.

Emotional intelligence is increased by focusing mental energy into a new perspective on emotions and behavior.

- The following pages deliver suggestions and specific actions you can take to improve your EQ.

Emotional intelligence is not learned in the same way you learn facts or information. Through the years, research has shown people learn emotional intelligence skills best when the following are present:

- A strong motivation to learn or change.
- Prolonged practice of new behaviors.
- Feedback on your behavior.

"I know of no more encouraging fact than the unquestionable ability of man to elevate his life by conscious endeavor."

- Henry David Thoreau

TAKING ACTION WITH EMOTIONAL INTELLIGENCE

Refer to the graph of your EQ skills on page 14 as you plan what to do with your results. Your best bet is to choose just one thing to work on first. You can move on to other skills once you've mastered the actionable steps for your first chosen skill.

Follow this two-step process:

1. Revisit the graph of your EQ skills on page 14 and your EQ goals on page 15.

2. Find your ACTION PLAN below.

If you want to improve your...

Self-Awareness .... turn to page 19

Self-Management .... turn to page 21

Social Awareness .... turn to page 24

Relationship Management .... turn to page 26

MAKING A CHANGE

When it comes to changing behavior, people can only focus effectively on a few things at a time. Therefore, it is best if you choose to focus on one EQ skill area at a time, pursuing the recommended actions for that skill.

How To Master A New Skill

When setting out to acquire a new skill, remember the best path for doing something new or different is the following:

- Find someone who is good at it.
- Watch that person do it.
- Ask that person to talk about how he or she does it.
- Practice doing it yourself with his or her guidance.
- Ask the person to give you feedback.
- Practice doing it on your own.
- Seek feedback until you've mastered it.

ACTION PLAN: SELF-AWARENESS

Self-Awareness is your ability to accurately recognize your emotions as they happen and to understand your general tendencies for responding to different people and situations.

	WHAT I SEE	WHAT I DO
WITH ME	Self-Awareness	Self-Management
WITH OTHERS	Social Awareness	Relationship Management

SELF-AWARENESS — *ACTION PLAN ONE*

To increase your Self-Awareness, practice watching your emotions like a hawk.

Step 1 Observe what you are feeling and doing **as the situation unfolds.**

- Don't wait until things go so far that your emotions make it hard for you to think about them objectively.

- Don't wait until the feeling goes away, either. Practice observing and recognizing your emotions in the moment to learn your response patterns.

Step 2 Monitor the thoughts and physical signs that **accompany a particular feeling.** These aren't the feelings themselves, but the thoughts and sensations that go with them:

• Do you sweat? • Does your heart beat fast? • Do you feel tense?	• Do your thoughts race? • Does your throat get tight? • Do you get tunnel vision?	• Does your mind go blank? • Do you shake? • Do you feel numb?

Step 3 Try to discover why you **react the way you do.**

- These responses to people and situations may be positive or negative.

- Why do you tend to react this way? What is it about the person or situation that elicits your response?

ACTION PLAN: SELF-AWARENESS

Self-Awareness is your ability to accurately recognize your emotions as they happen and to understand your general tendencies for responding to different people and situations.

	WHAT I SEE	WHAT I DO
WITH ME	Self-Awareness	Self-Management
WITH OTHERS	Social Awareness	Relationship Management

SELF-AWARENESS — *ACTION PLAN TWO*

Track your tendencies in different emotionally arousing situations.

Step 1 Record trends you see in your own behavior. **Literally write down what you see.**

- This requires taking an honest look at what you are thinking and feeling. After an emotionally arousing situation, sit down, think about it and record your response before you forget.

Step 2 Discover what negative behaviors you fall victim to when your emotions get the best of you. **Ask someone you trust to observe you and give you feedback.**

You may find that you:

• Make decisions you regret. • Interrupt people and/or are compelled to speak out.	• Try to escape the situation. • Fidget. • Avoid eye contact.	• Cry at inappropriate times. • Raise your voice. • Doubt yourself.

Step 3 Don't be afraid of your **emotional "mistakes."**

- The surprising thing about increasing Self-Awareness is that just thinking about it will help you change, even though you are focusing on things you do "wrong."

- Ineffective emotional responses usually happen beneath our awareness. If you understand your tendencies, you are more likely to choose a better response.

ACTION PLAN: SELF-MANAGEMENT

Self-Management is your ability to keep a pulse on your emotions so that you stay flexible and positively choose how you react to different situations and people.

	WHAT I SEE	WHAT I DO
WITH ME	Self-Awareness	Self-Management
WITH OTHERS	Social Awareness	Relationship Management

SELF-MANAGEMENT — *ACTION PLAN ONE*

Take an honest look at when you are being overwhelmed by your feelings.

Step 1 We all run into situations where our **emotions get the best of us.** Discover what these situations are for you.

You may feel:

● Passive ● Impulsive ● Frustrated	● Intense ● Oblivious ● Spaced-out	● Jazzed ● Restless ● Exhausted	● Numb ● Confused ● Distracted

Jot down a couple of situations where you catch your emotions getting the better of you:

Step 2 Learn to notice when you are feeling the emotions in Step 1. Admit what's happening, and **buy yourself some time before taking action.**

- Your thinking, your decisions and your actions are greatly influenced by your emotions. When your emotions are strong, you need to slow down and think before moving forward.

- Ignoring or minimizing what you are feeling is a guaranteed way to let your emotions control the situation.

ACTION PLAN: SELF-MANAGEMENT

Self-Management is your ability to keep a pulse on your emotions so that you stay flexible and positively choose how you react to different situations and people.

	WHAT I SEE	WHAT I DO
WITH ME	Self-Awareness	Self-Management
WITH OTHERS	Social Awareness	Relationship Management

SELF-MANAGEMENT — *ACTION PLAN TWO*

Take the reins and quit letting your emotions lead you around.

Step 1 Use strategies that help you **manage your reactions to emotionally arousing situations.**

Try these in the moment:

- **Listen** — During difficult conversations, always let the other party finish speaking, even if it takes a while. This greatly decreases your chances of rushing to judgment, calms the other person down and gives you time to think about what to do.

- **Step Back** — Picture the current situation in your head as if it weren't happening to you. If you were watching this in a movie, what would you recommend the main character (you) do to get the best results? An objective look at the situation will help you to think clearly, decreasing the chances you'll be led around by your emotions.

- **Breathe** — When all else fails, breathe! Whether you are happy, sad, anxious or mad, focusing your attention on gradual, deep, even-paced breaths will relax your body and clear your mind. When your head is clear you are more able to see and choose the best course of action.

Step 2 Use these strategies for the long term. They are great for problems that take time to solve.

- **Set aside** some time in your day for problem solving. Decisions made while hurrying through the day are seldom as effective as those made during moments of clarity.

- **Think** about where your emotion is coming from. If you are angry with someone, it is probably because she or he crossed a boundary with you. This boundary is as much about you as it is about them. Keep this in mind as you choose your course of action.

- **Plan** where you might be headed if you choose different courses of action. Plans based solely on an emotional reaction will lead you down the wrong path.

ACTION PLAN: SELF-MANAGEMENT

Self-Management is your ability to keep a pulse on your emotions so that you stay flexible and positively choose how you react to different situations and people.

	WHAT I SEE	WHAT I DO
WITH ME	Self-Awareness	Self-Management
WITH OTHERS	Social Awareness	Relationship Management

SELF-MANAGEMENT — *ACTION PLAN THREE*

Get ready for change because it is waiting around the corner.

Step 1 Prepare yourself for change **rather than ignoring it when it's on the way.**

- When anticipating change, talk through your concerns with a third party who is not as invested in the situation. Their perspective should help you pick up what you are missing rather than avoiding it.

Step 2 Work on being **flexible and adaptive** in the face of change.

- When change happens, admit to yourself that you can't change the reality that things are now different.

- The only thing you have control over is how you react to the new circumstances.

Step 3 Decide what you can do to **make the uninvited changes in your life produce what you want.**

- Make a list of potential positive outcomes that still exist despite the change.

- Use this list to keep you motivated as you work to achieve your goals.

ACTION PLAN: SOCIAL AWARENESS

Social Awareness is your ability to recognize and understand the moods of other individuals and entire groups of people. This awareness is necessary to control your reactions to others and manage relationships to the best of your ability.

	WHAT I SEE	WHAT I DO
WITH ME	Self-Awareness	Self-Management
WITH OTHERS	Social Awareness	Relationship Management

SOCIAL AWARENESS — *ACTION PLAN ONE*

When you are with other people, play anthropologist.

Step 1 When around people, spend extra time **observing, asking and listening.**

- Anthropologists often watch people in their natural state without letting their own thoughts and feelings disturb the interaction.

- Continue to spend time with others as you normally would, but keep "surveillance" on your mind. You will be surprised what you notice about others when your mind is more on them than it is on you.

Step 2 See if you can make a connection between what **the other person is feeling and what he or she is doing.**

- Be sure to ask lots of questions when you aren't sure.

Step 3 Don't forget to **pick up on the mood of the entire group.**

- If you look hard enough, you will often notice a mood in the room. It's a lot like picking up on the mood of an individual, except you'll see similarities between different people in the same group.

ACTION PLAN: SOCIAL AWARENESS

Social Awareness is your ability to recognize and understand the moods of other individuals and entire groups of people. This awareness is necessary to control your reactions to others and manage relationships to the best of your ability.

	WHAT I SEE	WHAT I DO
WITH ME	Self-Awareness	Self-Management
WITH OTHERS	Social Awareness	Relationship Management

SOCIAL AWARENESS — *ACTION PLAN TWO*

Check in with someone to see if you are accurately noticing what she or he is feeling.

Step 1 Seek out trusted friends or colleagues with whom you can **have a frank conversation with about your quest for improved Social Awareness.**

- The next time they tell you about something they experienced or something that is important to them, check in on the following:

  - Tell them your perception of what they are going through and see if it is accurate.

  - Don't be afraid to ask the kinds of questions you really can't ask during a typical conversation.

  - Finally, ask them if they were attempting to deliver any unspoken messages. Sometimes, people don't want to say flat out how they feel about something, so they drop hints. If they did, this is a great opportunity to see if you picked up on them.

Step 2 Finally, **repeat this process in a group setting.**

- Seek out a trusted friend or colleague with whom you've spent some time interacting in a group setting (a business meeting or a social dinner are perfect examples).

- Next time you are both in a group situation, tell him or her what you think is going on between people or with the group to check to see if he or she sees the same thing.

ACTION PLAN: RELATIONSHIP MANAGEMENT

Relationship Management is your ability to use your awareness of your emotions and the emotions of others to manage interactions and relationships constructively and to positive outcomes.

	WHAT I SEE	WHAT I DO
WITH ME	Self-Awareness	Self-Management
WITH OTHERS	Social Awareness	Relationship Management

RELATIONSHIP MANAGEMENT — *ACTION PLAN ONE*

Discover the role emotions play in *every* situation.

Step 1 Try to discover what role emotions are **playing in your interactions with others.**

- Understand that emotions play a part in every interaction between two people.

- Whether the mood is good or bad, excited or bored, think about how it is influencing the "back and forth" between you and another person.

Step 2 Spot when your emotions are **making things difficult.**

- Discussions, debates and negotiations sometimes stall for no apparent reason. Things usually fall flat when personal attachment is getting in the way of resolution.

- You will continue to argue until you address your interest or other emotional involvement in the difficult topic.

- When it's the other person who's emotional, address what they are feeling without being threatening or making him or her defensive.

Step 3 When you care, **show it.**

- When you have genuine interest in someone, don't hide it, even if there are only certain things you like about the person. People like people who like them.

- Always save time for small talk. A little bit of effort goes a long way here.

- Balance sharing yourself with asking questions about the other person. One-sided conversations turn people off and work against a real connection.

ACTION PLAN: RELATIONSHIP MANAGEMENT

Relationship Management is your ability to use your awareness of your emotions and the emotions of others to manage interactions and relationships constructively and to positive outcomes.

	WHAT I SEE	WHAT I DO
WITH ME	Self-Awareness	Self-Management
WITH OTHERS	Social Awareness	Relationship Management

RELATIONSHIP MANAGEMENT — *ACTION PLAN TWO*

Get real feedback on relationships from someone you trust.

Step 1 Seek out a trusted friend or colleague and get some **real feedback on how you're doing.**

- A "real" feedback discussion is bound to have some difficult moments, so you need to find someone with whom you can work through these moments comfortably.

- Explain to your selected person that you are working on Relationship Management as part of your Emotional Intelligence Appraisal™. Tell them what Relationship Management is and describe some of your goals for improving this skill.

Step 2 Ask this person to **share with you what he or she sees and thinks.** Be sure to get information on things that aren't readily apparent to you.

- The following questions should help this conversation:

  - What do I have a knack for that helps me get along with other people?

  - Is there a way I could use this skill more often or with different people?

  - What holds me back from relating as well as I could to others?

  - Are there specific situations where, or people with whom, I tend to make this mistake?

  - Is there anything I do too much of? That is, can I tone down a certain behavior?

A Final Note About Change

Change can often be hard. What you are about to work on may feel embarrassing or frustrating at times.

Change can be a little...

Embarrassing because as you practice new things, the very people who feel you ought to change may poke fun at you, forget to encourage you along the way, or not even notice. Don't give up. The rewards will far outweigh these challenges.

Frustrating because old habits and behaviors (what you say and do) can be difficult to change.

Change can also be terrific. Most are surprised how a little bit of change in the right direction can go a long way in the eyes of others. Good luck and have fun with it!

> "Human beings, by changing the inner attitudes of their minds, can change the outer aspects of their lives."
> – William James

WANT TO LEARN MORE ABOUT EQ?

READ THE EMOTIONAL INTELLIGENCE QUICKBOOK!

AVAILABLE EVERYWHERE BOOKS ARE SOLD FOR JUST $19.95

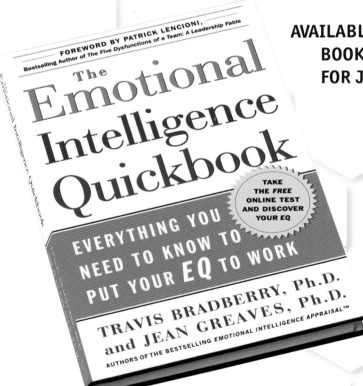

"What distinguishes human beings is that we are capable of positive change. This book succinctly explains how to deal with emotions creatively and employ our intelligence in a beneficial way."
~THE DALAI LAMA

"Research shows convincingly that EQ is more important than IQ. Gives abundant, practical findings and insights with emphasis on how to develop EQ."
~ STEPHEN R. COVEY, AUTHOR
THE 7 HABITS OF HIGHLY EFFECTIVE PEOPLE

"This book is excellent and the learning included with the free online survey is cutting-edge. I strongly recommend it."
~ KEN BLANCHARD, COAUTHOR
THE ONE MINUTE MANAGER®